Living Things and Their Habitats

Welcome to the Arctic

by Honor Head

Ruby Tuesday Books

Published in 2017 by Ruby Tuesday Books Ltd.

Editor: Jean Coppendale
Designer: Emma Randall
Consultant: Sally Morgan
Production: John Lingham

Photo credits
Alamy: 6 (bottom), 9, 15 (bottom), 17 (bottom), 18; Creative Commons: 14; FLPA: 7 (top), 8, 13 (left), 15 (top), 16 (bottom), 17 (top), 19, 28 (bottom), 29; Getty Images: 6 (top), 26; Nature Picture Library: 25; Shutterstock: Cover, 2–3, 4–5, 10–11, 12, 13 (right), 16 (top), 20–21, 22–23, 24, 27, 28 (top), 30–31; Superstock: 7 (bottom).

British Library Cataloguing in Publication Data (CIP) is available for this title.

ISBN 978-1-911341-51-2

Printed in China by Toppan Leefung

www.rubytuesdaybooks.com

Contents

Words shown in **bold** in the text are explained in the glossary.

Welcome to the Arctic

The Arctic is one of the coldest places on Earth.

It is made up of a large ocean surrounded by flat, treeless land called **tundra**.

This icy **habitat** is home to polar bears, whales, birds, insects and plants.

The Arctic tundra has many different ecosystems. An ecosystem includes all the living things in an area. It also includes non-living things such as the sea, ice, snow and sun. Everything in an ecosystem has its own part to play.

The Arctic is in the most northern part of the world.

Arctic Ocean

Snow-covered tundra

The Arctic Ocean is so cold that part of its surface is always frozen.

Sometimes in winter, this vast floating island of thick ice spreads and joins up with the land.

Let's find out what happens in this habitat.
Welcome to the Arctic!

Life in the Freezing Ocean

The Arctic Ocean may be icy, but it's filled with life.

Seals dive below the floating ice to hunt.

They use their flippers to twist and turn as they chase squid and fish.

Seal

Ice floating on the ocean surface

Frozen ocean

Seals use their claws or teeth to make breathing holes in the ice where they can come up for air.

Breathing hole

Walruses use their sensitive whiskers to feel for clams, mussels and other **prey** on the ocean floor.

Whiskers

Walrus

Tusk

Ice floe

Walruses have two extra-long teeth called tusks.

They use their tusks to pull themselves up onto **ice floes** when they want to rest.

Who is hunting for seals on the frozen ocean?

Frozen Winter

The Arctic winter starts in November.

Polar bears hunt for seals on the frozen ocean.

When a polar bear finds a seal's breathing hole, it waits very still by the hole.

When the seal comes up for air, the polar bear grabs it.

Seal

Breathing hole

A hungry Arctic fox follows its big, fierce neighbour.

Once the bear has finished feeding, the little fox will eat the leftovers.

During the Arctic winter there are fierce **blizzards** of freezing, icy snow. The temperature falls to −40 degrees Celsius. The tundra is frozen and no plants grow.

Arctic fox

Who is sleeping under the snow?

A Den in the Snow

In autumn, a pregnant female polar bear digs a den in the snow.

Then she climbs inside and goes to sleep.

Snow covers the entrance to the den.

The polar bear is warm and safe inside.

During the winter, the bear gives birth to tiny twin cubs.

A polar bear inside her den

Newborn polar bear cubs are the size of a guinea pig. They have no teeth and they cannot see.

The baby bears drink milk from their mother's body.

Polar bear cub

What happens when spring sunshine warms up the tundra?

The Big Melt

When spring comes, the warm sun starts to melt the snow and ice.

The water makes small ponds, lakes and soggy **marshes** on the tundra.

Musk oxen

Mosquitoes lay their eggs in the ponds and marshes. The mosquitoes feed on the blood of polar bears, musk oxen, reindeer and other animals.

Mosquito

Small, low-growing plants, such as moss, grasses, heather and Arctic willow, grow.

A lemming eating flowers

The plants' leaves, flowers, fruits and seeds are food for Arctic animals.

An Arctic ground squirrel eating seeds

Which furry little insect is waking up now that spring has arrived?

Small Wonders

In early spring, a woolly bear caterpillar wakes up from **hibernation**.

During its long winter sleep, the caterpillar freezes solid. Special chemicals in its body allow the caterpillar to freeze but not die. Once the spring sunshine warms its body, the caterpillar defrosts and becomes active!

A woolly bear caterpillar warming up on a sunny rock.

Arctic willow

The caterpillar feeds on the new leaves of Arctic willow plants.

It eats for about three weeks.

Then it goes back into hibernation for another year.

The caterpillar does this for up to 14 years, until it is ready to change into a moth.

Once it's a moth, the insect only lives for a few days – just long enough to **mate** and lay eggs.

Who has hungry babies to feed on the tundra?

Babies on the Tundra

An Arctic fox is hunting for birds, lemmings and other small animals on the tundra.

Arctic fox

She brings this food to her pups.

An Arctic fox's fur colour is good **camouflage** that helps it hide from **predators**, such as polar bears and wolves. In winter, the fox's fur is white, like snow. In spring, the fox grows a brownish-grey coat.

A pup eating a bird

The Arctic fox pups play fight to learn how to hunt and protect themselves.

In spring, a pair of snowy owls digs a shallow nest on the tundra.

Snowy owl

Chick

The parent owls catch lemmings and mice to feed to their chicks.

Which baby animals must make a long, dangerous journey?

Babies on the Ice

The polar bear cubs are now old enough to leave their den.

The mother bear is hungry because she hasn't eaten for many months.

The family must make a long walk to the sea to find seals to eat.

In some parts of the Arctic, it is icy and snowy even in spring and summer.

The mother bear must keep watch for male polar bears or wolves that might attack and eat her cubs.

Harp seals give birth to their babies on the sea ice.

Mother seal

Harp seal pup

The seal pups have white coats so that hungry polar bears cannot see them on the ice.

What animals are fishing in the icy ocean?

19

Fish Feast

The Arctic coastline is a good place for seabirds to raise their chicks.

The ocean is teeming with fish, so there is plenty of food to feed the baby birds.

Kittiwakes build their nests from plants and seaweed stuck together with mud.

Kittiwakes and puffins make their nests on steep cliffs. It is difficult for predators, such as Arctic foxes, to steal the eggs and chicks.

Chick

Kittiwake

A male puffin uses his beak and feet to dig a **burrow** in the ground.

His partner lays a single egg inside.

Puffins dive into the ocean to catch small fish, called sand eels, to feed to their chicks.

Puffin

Sand eels

Puffins on a clifftop

Burrow

Burrow

What giant animals are feeding in the Arctic Ocean?

Whale Watch

Huge humpback whales glide through the Arctic Ocean.

To catch food, a humpback whale dives down into the water.

As it swims back up to the surface, it opens its mouth wide.

Humpback whale

It takes in a mouthful of water and food.

Then the whale closes its mouth and squeezes the water out through its baleen plates.

The humpback now has a mouthful of tasty food.

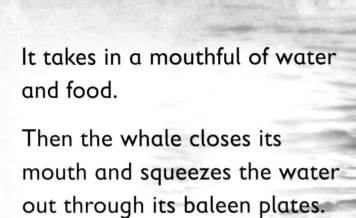

A whale's open mouth

Tongue

Baleen plate

Humpback whales feast on tiny animals called **krill**, and fish such as herring and mackerel.

Krill

Which hungry ocean animals are hunting as a team?

On the Hunt

An orca looking for a seal

Families of orcas, or killer whales, live and hunt in the Arctic Ocean.

Orcas have a clever way of catching seals, called seal washing.

Seal

A group of orcas spots a seal resting on an ice floe.

When hunting, orcas send clicking and calling noises to one another. The noises tell each member of the team what is happening and what to do.

The orcas form a line and swim fast towards the ice floe.

Orcas creating a wave

Their underwater charge creates two big waves.

The first wave tips up the ice floe and the second wave washes the seal into the sea.

Why are huge herds of reindeer heading to the tundra?

A Great Migration

Thousands of caribou, or reindeer, spend the winter in the forests at the edge of the tundra.

In summer, they **migrate** to the tundra to feed on plants.

A herd of migrating caribou

Herds of migrating caribou can stretch for more than 300 kilometres. They follow trails that have been used for hundreds of years.

As they migrate, the female caribou give birth to their calves.

By the end of its first day, a caribou calf can run faster than a human.

A one-day-old calf

Wolf

A four-month-old calf

The little calf must be able to run from wolves that follow the caribou herds.

Caribou feeding on the tundra.

Why is the air growing much colder?

Winter Returns

Spring, summer and autumn are short in the Arctic.

Soon it grows much colder and heavy snow falls.

A nine-month-old cub

Mother bear

The polar bear cubs are learning how to hunt seals.

Lemming

A lemming stays warm in its burrow under the snow.

In winter, there's not much food around. Arctic foxes feed on the remains of dead animals. They will even eat polar bear poo if they find some!

Arctic fox

A hungry Arctic fox goes hunting.

When it hears a lemming under the snow, it dives in to catch its meal.

Icy winds and blizzards blast the tundra. Winter has returned to the Arctic!

29

An Arctic Food Web

A food web shows who eats who in a habitat.

This food web shows the connections between some of the living things in the Arctic.

Plants make the food they need for energy inside themselves. To do this, they need sunlight.

Seal

Polar bear

Arctic fox

Snowy owl

Fish

The arrows mean:
eaten by

Krill

Plants

Lemming

Glossary

blizzard
A very heavy snowstorm with strong winds.

burrow
A hole or tunnel that an animal digs as a home.

camouflage
Colours or markings that help an animal blend into its habitat.

habitat
The place where a living thing, such as a plant or animal, makes its home. The tundra, ocean and deserts are all types of habitats.

hibernation
Spending the winter in a deep sleep.

ice floe
A chunk of floating ice.

krill
Tiny shrimp-like animals that live in the ocean.

marsh
An area of land where there is lots of water in the soil, so the ground is very soft and wet.

mate
To get together to produce young.

migrate
To move a long way from one place to another. Animals might migrate to find food or to get away from very cold or very hot weather.

predator
An animal that hunts and eats other animals.

prey
An animal that is hunted by other animals for food.

tundra
A flat, rocky, treeless landscape of low-growing plants. Below the surface the soil is always frozen.

Index

A
Arctic foxes 9, 16–17, 20, 29, 30
Arctic ground squirrel 13

B
birds 4, 16–17, 20–21, 30

C
camouflage 16, 19
caribou (reindeer) 12, 25, 26–27

F
fish 6, 20–21, 23, 30

I
insects 4, 12–13, 14–15

K
kittiwakes 20
krill 23, 30

L
lemmings 13, 16–17, 28–29, 30

M
mosquitoes 12
musk oxen 12

O
orcas 24–25

P
plants 4, 9, 13, 15, 20, 26, 30
polar bears 4, 8–9, 10–11, 12, 16, 18–19, 28–29, 30
predators and prey 6–7, 8–9, 16–17, 18–19, 20–21, 23, 24–25, 27, 28–29, 30
puffins 20–21

S
seals 6–7, 8, 18–19, 24–25, 28, 30
snowy owls 4, 17, 30

W
walruses 7
whales 4, 22–23, 24–25
wolves 16, 19, 27
woolly bear caterpillars 14–15

Learn More Online

To learn more about life in the Arctic, go to
www.rubytuesdaybooks.com/habitats